Just TO DO IT

By Free Life Compass

How to Organize Your Life

1. Write it Down

Make a new to-do list every day based on the previous day's list and all that came up since the last list was created.

2. Three ways.

Three lists way: 1 - master list, with every item you'd like to accomplish in the long-term. 2- can be a weekly project list. 3 - high-impact tasks list, with the tasks that need to get done today.

3. Simplify.

There's nothing more intimidating than a mile-long to-do list. Make it simple and reasonable. It is 24 hours in a day.

4. Most Important to you.

Highlight at least two items that absolutely must get done today.

5. Easy start.

Start list with few simple tasks. Even crossing off silly stuff helps us start the day feeling super-productive.

6. Break it down.

If you describe goals too vague it will be intimidating, meaning we'll be too afraid to actually start doing them. Make goals seem more manageable, break projects into smaller tasks.

7. Stay specific.

All to-do's meant to be: physical actions; they can be finished in one sitting; and they're tasks that only the to-do-list writer can do.

8. No stress.

If you have a few tasks on list that you have been meaning to do for days, weeks, maybe even years – but haven't yet (!), try to figure out why not (?) in order to learn what steps are necessary for actually completing the task.

9. Keep it.

One way to boost productivity is to remind ourselves how productive we were yesterday. So keep a written list of everything you accomplished the day before, even the small stuff.

10. Be flexible.

Always leave about 15 minutes of No stress Time in between items on the to-do list or calendar in case something pops up.

Remember - you have it under control!

TO - DO

- [ ]
- [ ]
- [ ]
- [ ]
- [ ]
- [ ]
- [ ]

- [ ]
- [ ]
- [ ]
- [ ]
- [ ]
- [ ]
- [ ]

GREAT JOB!

TO - DO

☐
☐
☐
☐
☐
☐
☐

☐
☐
☐
☐
☐
☐

GREAT JOB!

TO - DO

☐

☐

☐

☐

☐

☐

☐

☐

☐

☐

☐

☐

☐

☐

GREAT JOB!

TO - DO

- [ ]
- [ ]
- [ ]
- [ ]
- [ ]
- [ ]
- [ ]

- [ ]
- [ ]
- [ ]
- [ ]
- [ ]
- [ ]

GREAT JOB!

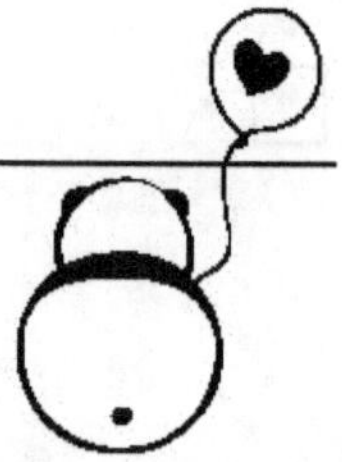

TO - DO

- [ ]
- [ ]
- [ ]
- [ ]
- [ ]
- [ ]
- [ ]

- [ ]
- [ ]
- [ ]
- [ ]
- [ ]
- [ ]

GREAT JOB!

TO - DO

- ☐
- ☐
- ☐
- ☐
- ☐
- ☐
- ☐

- ☐
- ☐
- ☐
- ☐
- ☐
- ☐
- ☐

GREAT JOB!

TO - DO

☐ ____________________

☐ ____________________

☐ ____________________

☐ ____________________

☐ ____________________

☐ ____________________

☐ ____________________

☐ ____________________

☐ ____________________

☐ ____________________

☐ ____________________

☐ ____________________

☐ ____________________

GREAT JOB!

TO - DO

- [ ]
- [ ]
- [ ]
- [ ]
- [ ]
- [ ]
- [ ]

- [ ]
- [ ]
- [ ]
- [ ]
- [ ]
- [ ]
- [ ]

GREAT JOB!

TO - DO

GREAT JOB!

TO - DO

- [ ]
- [ ]
- [ ]
- [ ]
- [ ]
- [ ]
- [ ]

- [ ]
- [ ]
- [ ]
- [ ]
- [ ]
- [ ]
- [ ]

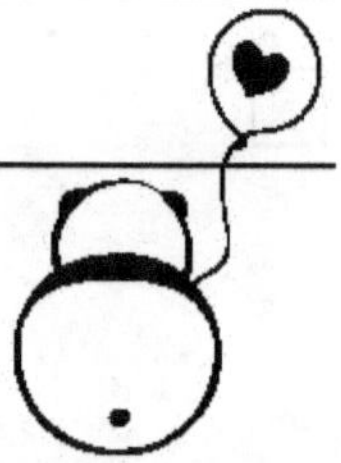

GREAT JOB!

TO - DO

GREAT JOB!

TO - DO

GREAT JOB!

TO - DO

- [ ]
- [ ]
- [ ]
- [ ]
- [ ]
- [ ]
- [ ]

- [ ]
- [ ]
- [ ]
- [ ]
- [ ]
- [ ]

GREAT JOB!

TO - DO

GREAT JOB!

TO - DO

- [ ]
- [ ]
- [ ]
- [ ]
- [ ]
- [ ]
- [ ]

- [ ]
- [ ]
- [ ]
- [ ]
- [ ]
- [ ]
- [ ]

GREAT JOB!

TO - DO

- [ ]
- [ ]
- [ ]
- [ ]
- [ ]
- [ ]
- [ ]

- [ ]
- [ ]
- [ ]
- [ ]
- [ ]
- [ ]
- [ ]

GREAT JOB!

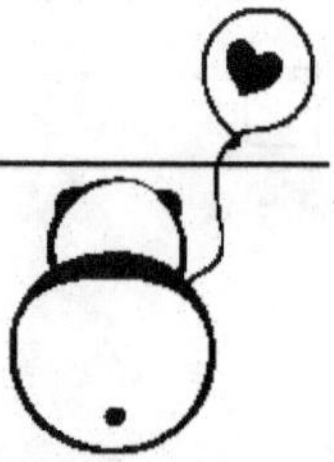

TO - DO

- [ ]
- [ ]
- [ ]
- [ ]
- [ ]
- [ ]
- [ ]

- [ ]
- [ ]
- [ ]
- [ ]
- [ ]
- [ ]
- [ ]

GREAT JOB!

TO - DO

- [ ]
- [ ]
- [ ]
- [ ]
- [ ]
- [ ]
- [ ]

- [ ]
- [ ]
- [ ]
- [ ]
- [ ]
- [ ]
- [ ]

GREAT JOB!

TO - DO

- [ ]
- [ ]
- [ ]
- [ ]
- [ ]
- [ ]
- [ ]

- [ ]
- [ ]
- [ ]
- [ ]
- [ ]
- [ ]

GREAT JOB!

TO - DO

- [ ]
- [ ]
- [ ]
- [ ]
- [ ]
- [ ]
- [ ]

- [ ]
- [ ]
- [ ]
- [ ]
- [ ]
- [ ]
- [ ]

GREAT JOB!

TO - DO

- [ ]
- [ ]
- [ ]
- [ ]
- [ ]
- [ ]
- [ ]

- [ ]
- [ ]
- [ ]
- [ ]
- [ ]
- [ ]
- [ ]

GREAT JOB!

TO - DO

- [ ]
- [ ]
- [ ]
- [ ]
- [ ]
- [ ]
- [ ]

- [ ]
- [ ]
- [ ]
- [ ]
- [ ]
- [ ]
- [ ]

GREAT JOB!

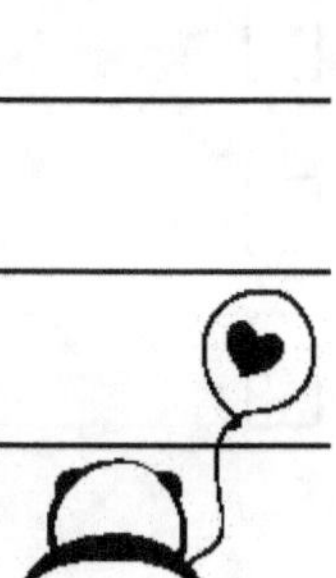

TO - DO

- [ ]
- [ ]
- [ ]
- [ ]
- [ ]
- [ ]
- [ ]

- [ ]
- [ ]
- [ ]
- [ ]
- [ ]
- [ ]

GREAT JOB!

TO - DO

- [ ]
- [ ]
- [ ]
- [ ]
- [ ]
- [ ]
- [ ]

- [ ]
- [ ]
- [ ]
- [ ]
- [ ]
- [ ]

GREAT JOB!

TO - DO

- [ ]
- [ ]
- [ ]
- [ ]
- [ ]
- [ ]
- [ ]

- [ ]
- [ ]
- [ ]
- [ ]
- [ ]
- [ ]
- [ ]

GREAT JOB!

TO - DO

- [ ]
- [ ]
- [ ]
- [ ]
- [ ]
- [ ]
- [ ]

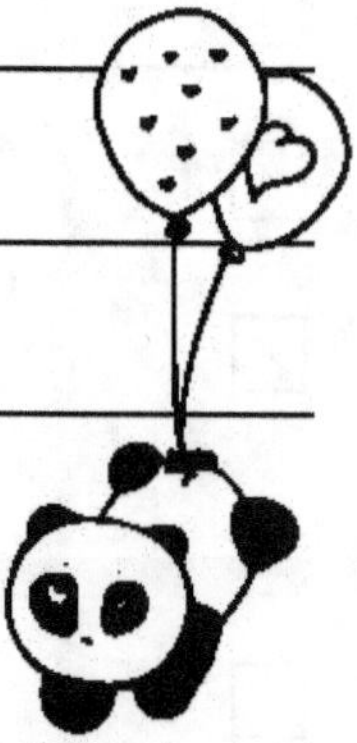

- [ ]
- [ ]
- [ ]
- [ ]
- [ ]
- [ ]
- [ ]

GREAT JOB!

TO - DO

- [ ]
- [ ]
- [ ]
- [ ]
- [ ]
- [ ]
- [ ]

- [ ]
- [ ]
- [ ]
- [ ]
- [ ]
- [ ]

GREAT JOB!

TO - DO

☐
☐
☐
☐
☐
☐
☐

☐
☐
☐
☐
☐
☐

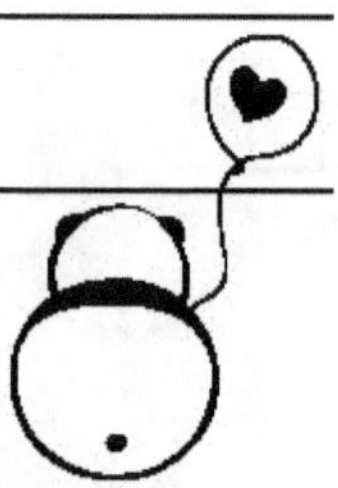

GREAT JOB!

TO - DO

☐ ______________________________

☐ ______________________________

☐ ______________________________

☐ ______________________________

☐ ______________________________

☐ ______________________________

☐ ______________________________

☐ ______________________________

☐ ______________________________

☐ ______________________________

☐ ______________________________

☐ ______________________________

☐ ______________________________

☐ ______________________________

GREAT JOB!

TO - DO

- [ ]
- [ ]
- [ ]
- [ ]
- [ ]
- [ ]
- [ ]

- [ ]
- [ ]
- [ ]
- [ ]
- [ ]
- [ ]

GREAT JOB!

TO - DO

- [ ]
- [ ]
- [ ]
- [ ]
- [ ]
- [ ]
- [ ]

- [ ]
- [ ]
- [ ]
- [ ]
- [ ]
- [ ]

GREAT JOB!

TO - DO

- [ ]
- [ ]
- [ ]
- [ ]
- [ ]
- [ ]
- [ ]

- [ ]
- [ ]
- [ ]
- [ ]
- [ ]
- [ ]
- [ ]

GREAT JOB!

TO - DO

- [ ]
- [ ]
- [ ]
- [ ]
- [ ]
- [ ]
- [ ]

- [ ]
- [ ]
- [ ]
- [ ]
- [ ]
- [ ]

GREAT JOB!

TO - DO

- [ ]
- [ ]
- [ ]
- [ ]
- [ ]
- [ ]
- [ ]

- [ ]
- [ ]
- [ ]
- [ ]
- [ ]
- [ ]
- [ ]

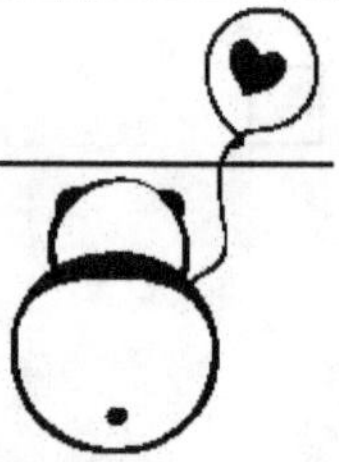

GREAT JOB!

TO - DO

- [ ]
- [ ]
- [ ]
- [ ]
- [ ]
- [ ]
- [ ]

- [ ]
- [ ]
- [ ]
- [ ]
- [ ]
- [ ]
- [ ]

GREAT JOB!

TO - DO

- [ ]
- [ ]
- [ ]
- [ ]
- [ ]
- [ ]
- [ ]

- [ ]
- [ ]
- [ ]
- [ ]
- [ ]
- [ ]
- [ ]

GREAT JOB!

TO - DO

- [ ]
- [ ]
- [ ]
- [ ]
- [ ]
- [ ]
- [ ]

- [ ]
- [ ]
- [ ]
- [ ]
- [ ]
- [ ]
- [ ]

GREAT JOB!

TO - DO

- [ ]
- [ ]
- [ ]
- [ ]
- [ ]
- [ ]
- [ ]

- [ ]
- [ ]
- [ ]
- [ ]
- [ ]
- [ ]
- [ ]

GREAT JOB!

TO - DO

- [ ]
- [ ]
- [ ]
- [ ]
- [ ]
- [ ]
- [ ]

- [ ]
- [ ]
- [ ]
- [ ]
- [ ]
- [ ]
- [ ]

GREAT JOB!

TO - DO

- [ ]
- [ ]
- [ ]
- [ ]
- [ ]
- [ ]
- [ ]

- [ ]
- [ ]
- [ ]
- [ ]
- [ ]
- [ ]

GREAT JOB!

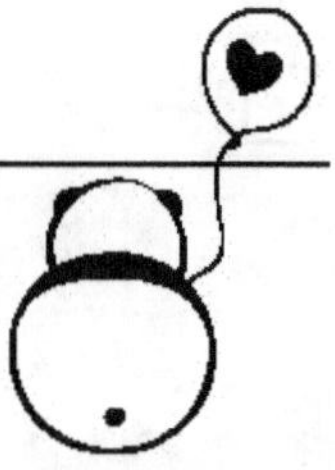

TO - DO

- [ ]
- [ ]
- [ ]
- [ ]
- [ ]
- [ ]
- [ ]

- [ ]
- [ ]
- [ ]
- [ ]
- [ ]
- [ ]

GREAT JOB!

TO - DO

☐

☐

☐

☐

☐

☐

☐

☐

☐

☐

☐

☐

☐

GREAT JOB!

TO - DO

GREAT JOB!

TO - DO

- [ ]
- [ ]
- [ ]
- [ ]
- [ ]
- [ ]
- [ ]

- [ ]
- [ ]
- [ ]
- [ ]
- [ ]
- [ ]
- [ ]

GREAT JOB!

TO - DO

- [ ]
- [ ]
- [ ]
- [ ]
- [ ]
- [ ]
- [ ]

- [ ]
- [ ]
- [ ]
- [ ]
- [ ]
- [ ]
- [ ]

GREAT JOB!

TO - DO

- [ ]
- [ ]
- [ ]
- [ ]
- [ ]
- [ ]
- [ ]

- [ ]
- [ ]
- [ ]
- [ ]
- [ ]
- [ ]
- [ ]

GREAT JOB!

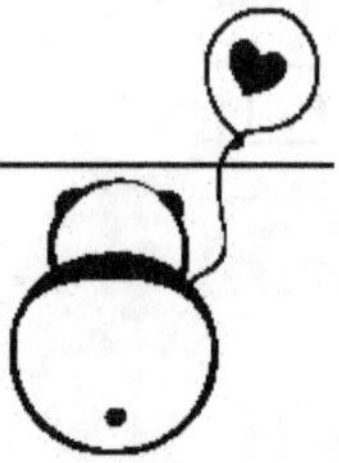

TO - DO

- [ ]
- [ ]
- [ ]
- [ ]
- [ ]
- [ ]
- [ ]

- [ ]
- [ ]
- [ ]
- [ ]
- [ ]
- [ ]
- [ ]

GREAT JOB!

TO - DO

☐

☐

☐

☐

☐

☐

☐

☐

☐

☐

☐

☐

☐

☐

GREAT JOB!

TO - DO

GREAT JOB!

TO - DO

☐
☐
☐
☐
☐
☐
☐

☐
☐
☐
☐
☐
☐

GREAT JOB!

TO - DO

- [ ]
- [ ]
- [ ]
- [ ]
- [ ]
- [ ]
- [ ]

- [ ]
- [ ]
- [ ]
- [ ]
- [ ]
- [ ]

GREAT JOB!

TO - DO

- [ ]
- [ ]
- [ ]
- [ ]
- [ ]
- [ ]
- [ ]

- [ ]
- [ ]
- [ ]
- [ ]
- [ ]
- [ ]

GREAT JOB!

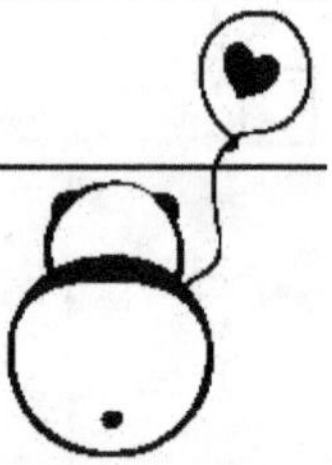

TO - DO

GREAT JOB!

TO - DO

☐

☐

☐

☐

☐

☐

☐

☐

☐

☐

☐

☐

☐

GREAT JOB!

TO - DO

- [ ]
- [ ]
- [ ]
- [ ]
- [ ]
- [ ]
- [ ]

- [ ]
- [ ]
- [ ]
- [ ]
- [ ]
- [ ]

GREAT JOB!

TO - DO

GREAT JOB!

TO - DO

- [ ]
- [ ]
- [ ]
- [ ]
- [ ]
- [ ]
- [ ]

- [ ]
- [ ]
- [ ]
- [ ]
- [ ]
- [ ]
- [ ]

GREAT JOB!

TO - DO

- [ ]
- [ ]
- [ ]
- [ ]
- [ ]
- [ ]
- [ ]

- [ ]
- [ ]
- [ ]
- [ ]
- [ ]
- [ ]
- [ ]

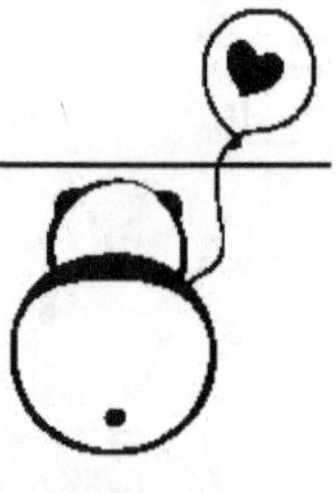

GREAT JOB!

TO - DO

- [ ]
- [ ]
- [ ]
- [ ]
- [ ]
- [ ]
- [ ]

- [ ]
- [ ]
- [ ]
- [ ]
- [ ]
- [ ]
- [ ]

GREAT JOB!

TO - DO

GREAT JOB!

TO - DO

- [ ]
- [ ]
- [ ]
- [ ]
- [ ]
- [ ]
- [ ]

- [ ]
- [ ]
- [ ]
- [ ]
- [ ]
- [ ]
- [ ]

GREAT JOB!

TO - DO

- [ ]
- [ ]
- [ ]
- [ ]
- [ ]
- [ ]
- [ ]

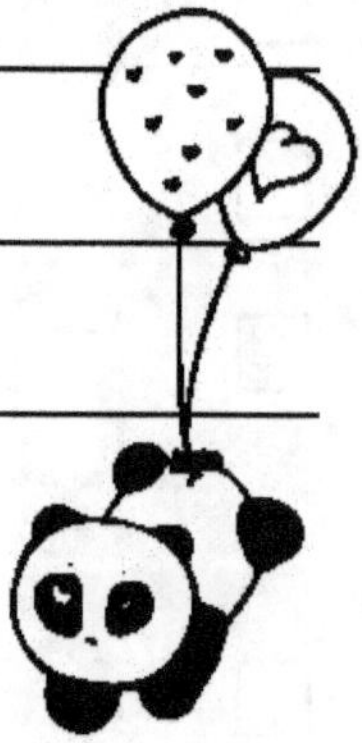

- [ ]
- [ ]
- [ ]
- [ ]
- [ ]
- [ ]
- [ ]

GREAT JOB!

TO - DO

- [ ]
- [ ]
- [ ]
- [ ]
- [ ]
- [ ]
- [ ]

- [ ]
- [ ]
- [ ]
- [ ]
- [ ]
- [ ]

GREAT JOB!

TO - DO

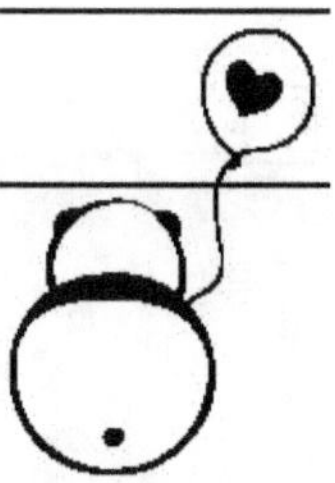

GREAT JOB!

TO - DO

- [ ]
- [ ]
- [ ]
- [ ]
- [ ]
- [ ]
- [ ]

- [ ]
- [ ]
- [ ]
- [ ]
- [ ]
- [ ]
- [ ]

GREAT JOB!

TO - DO

☐

☐

☐

☐

☐

☐

☐

☐

☐

☐

☐

☐

☐

☐

GREAT JOB!

TO - DO

- [ ]
- [ ]
- [ ]
- [ ]
- [ ]
- [ ]
- [ ]

- [ ]
- [ ]
- [ ]
- [ ]
- [ ]
- [ ]

GREAT JOB!

TO - DO

- [ ]
- [ ]
- [ ]
- [ ]
- [ ]
- [ ]
- [ ]

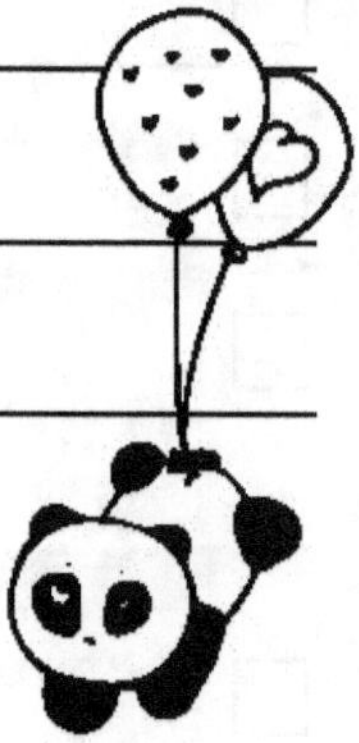

- [ ]
- [ ]
- [ ]
- [ ]
- [ ]
- [ ]
- [ ]

GREAT JOB!

TO - DO

- [ ]
- [ ]
- [ ]
- [ ]
- [ ]
- [ ]
- [ ]

- [ ]
- [ ]
- [ ]
- [ ]
- [ ]
- [ ]
- [ ]

GREAT JOB!

TO - DO

- [ ]
- [ ]
- [ ]
- [ ]
- [ ]
- [ ]
- [ ]

- [ ]
- [ ]
- [ ]
- [ ]
- [ ]
- [ ]
- [ ]

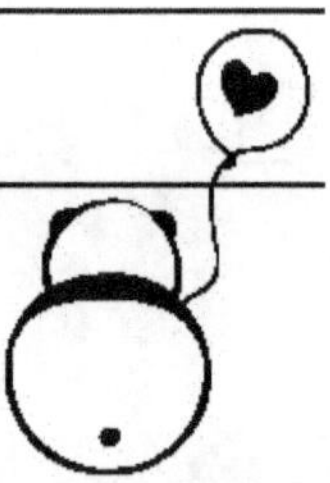

GREAT JOB!

TO - DO

GREAT JOB!

TO - DO

- [ ]
- [ ]
- [ ]
- [ ]
- [ ]
- [ ]
- [ ]

- [ ]
- [ ]
- [ ]
- [ ]
- [ ]
- [ ]
- [ ]

GREAT JOB!

TO - DO

- [ ]
- [ ]
- [ ]
- [ ]
- [ ]
- [ ]
- [ ]

- [ ]
- [ ]
- [ ]
- [ ]
- [ ]
- [ ]
- [ ]

GREAT JOB!

TO - DO

- [ ]
- [ ]
- [ ]
- [ ]
- [ ]
- [ ]
- [ ]

- [ ]
- [ ]
- [ ]
- [ ]
- [ ]
- [ ]
- [ ]

GREAT JOB!

TO - DO

- [ ]
- [ ]
- [ ]
- [ ]
- [ ]
- [ ]
- [ ]

- [ ]
- [ ]
- [ ]
- [ ]
- [ ]
- [ ]
- [ ]

GREAT JOB!

TO - DO

- [ ]
- [ ]
- [ ]
- [ ]
- [ ]
- [ ]
- [ ]

- [ ]
- [ ]
- [ ]
- [ ]
- [ ]
- [ ]

GREAT JOB!

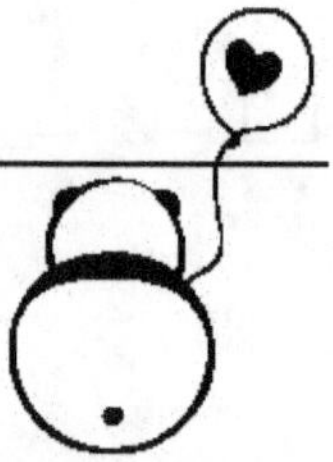

TO - DO

☐

☐

☐

☐

☐

☐

☐

☐

☐

☐

☐

☐

☐

GREAT JOB!

TO - DO

- [ ]
- [ ]
- [ ]
- [ ]
- [ ]
- [ ]
- [ ]

- [ ]
- [ ]
- [ ]
- [ ]
- [ ]
- [ ]

GREAT JOB!

TO - DO

- [ ]
- [ ]
- [ ]
- [ ]
- [ ]
- [ ]
- [ ]

- [ ]
- [ ]
- [ ]
- [ ]
- [ ]
- [ ]
- [ ]

GREAT JOB!

TO - DO

GREAT JOB!

TO - DO

- [ ]
- [ ]
- [ ]
- [ ]
- [ ]
- [ ]
- [ ]

- [ ]
- [ ]
- [ ]
- [ ]
- [ ]
- [ ]
- [ ]

GREAT JOB!

TO - DO

GREAT JOB!

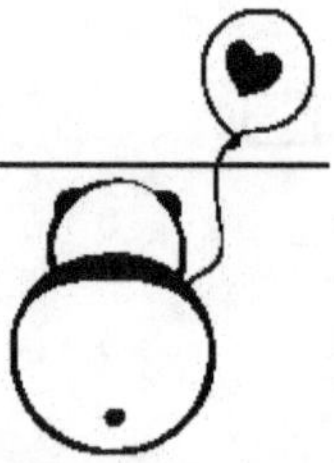

TO - DO

- [ ]
- [ ]
- [ ]
- [ ]
- [ ]
- [ ]
- [ ]

- [ ]
- [ ]
- [ ]
- [ ]
- [ ]
- [ ]
- [ ]

GREAT JOB!

TO - DO

- [ ]
- [ ]
- [ ]
- [ ]
- [ ]
- [ ]
- [ ]

- [ ]
- [ ]
- [ ]
- [ ]
- [ ]
- [ ]

GREAT JOB!

TO - DO

- [ ]
- [ ]
- [ ]
- [ ]
- [ ]
- [ ]
- [ ]

- [ ]
- [ ]
- [ ]
- [ ]
- [ ]
- [ ]

GREAT JOB!

TO - DO

- [ ]
- [ ]
- [ ]
- [ ]
- [ ]
- [ ]
- [ ]

- [ ]
- [ ]
- [ ]
- [ ]
- [ ]
- [ ]
- [ ]

GREAT JOB!

TO - DO

- [ ]
- [ ]
- [ ]
- [ ]
- [ ]
- [ ]
- [ ]

- [ ]
- [ ]
- [ ]
- [ ]
- [ ]
- [ ]
- [ ]

GREAT JOB!

TO - DO

GREAT JOB!

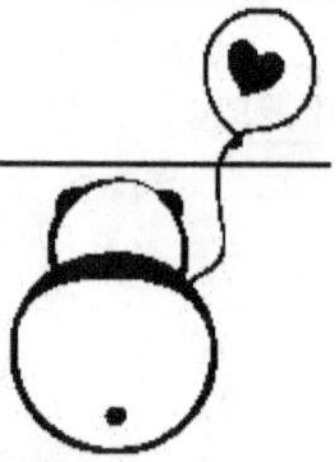

TO - DO

GREAT JOB!

TO - DO

- [ ]
- [ ]
- [ ]
- [ ]
- [ ]
- [ ]
- [ ]

- [ ]
- [ ]
- [ ]
- [ ]
- [ ]
- [ ]
- [ ]

GREAT JOB!

TO - DO

- [ ]
- [ ]
- [ ]
- [ ]
- [ ]
- [ ]
- [ ]

- [ ]
- [ ]
- [ ]
- [ ]
- [ ]
- [ ]
- [ ]

GREAT JOB!

TO - DO

- [ ]
- [ ]
- [ ]
- [ ]
- [ ]
- [ ]
- [ ]

- [ ]
- [ ]
- [ ]
- [ ]
- [ ]
- [ ]
- [ ]

GREAT JOB!

TO - DO

- [ ]
- [ ]
- [ ]
- [ ]
- [ ]
- [ ]
- [ ]

- [ ]
- [ ]
- [ ]
- [ ]
- [ ]
- [ ]

GREAT JOB!

TO - DO

- [ ]
- [ ]
- [ ]
- [ ]
- [ ]
- [ ]
- [ ]

- [ ]
- [ ]
- [ ]
- [ ]
- [ ]
- [ ]
- [ ]

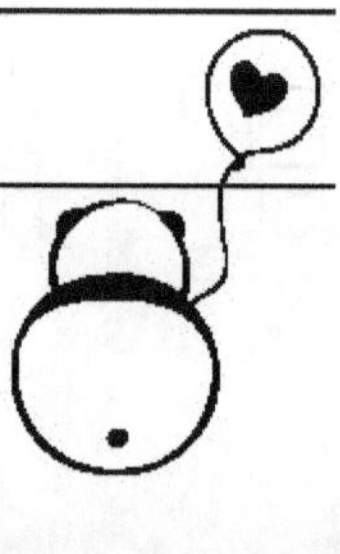

GREAT JOB!

TO - DO

GREAT JOB!

TO - DO

GREAT JOB!

TO - DO

- [ ]
- [ ]
- [ ]
- [ ]
- [ ]
- [ ]
- [ ]

- [ ]
- [ ]
- [ ]
- [ ]
- [ ]
- [ ]
- [ ]

GREAT JOB!

TO - DO

GREAT JOB!

TO - DO

☐ ____________________

☐ ____________________

☐ ____________________

☐ ____________________

☐ ____________________

☐ ____________________

☐ ____________________

☐ ____________________

☐ ____________________

☐ ____________________

☐ ____________________

☐ ____________________

☐ ____________________

☐ ____________________

GREAT JOB!

TO - DO

☐

☐

☐

☐

☐

☐

☐

☐

☐

☐

☐

☐

☐

☐

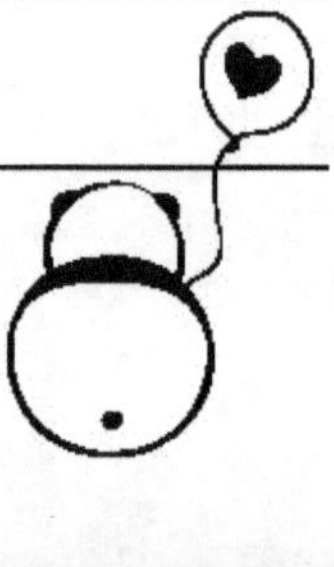

GREAT JOB!

TO - DO

- [ ]
- [ ]
- [ ]
- [ ]
- [ ]
- [ ]
- [ ]

- [ ]
- [ ]
- [ ]
- [ ]
- [ ]
- [ ]
- [ ]

GREAT JOB!

www.ingramcontent.com/pod-product-compliance
Lightning Source LLC
Chambersburg PA
CBHW072225170526
45158CB00002BA/756
* 9 7 8 1 0 8 2 0 0 2 1 3 7 *